GROWING
DELI‹

CW01509588

Step By Step Beginners Instruction To The Complete Growing Techniques & Troubleshooting Solutions

SHANE BOWIE

Table of Contents

Introductory

The flowering plant Monstera deliciosa, or Swiss cheese plant, is indigenous to the tropical rainforests of southern Mexico and the Caribbean coast all the way to Panama. Large, glossy green leaves with unusual splits and holes, resembling Swiss cheese, make this Araceae plant stand out. The plant's lovely and distinctive foliage makes it a popular option for houseplants and other interior décor.

As a climbing plant, Monstera deliciosa is capable of growing in either a vertical or horizontal orientation. In its native environment, it frequently alights atop trees and other man-made buildings. Under ideal circumstances, this plant can yield edible fruit, which is where the term "deliciosa" comes from.

Popular names for this fruit include "Monstera fruit" and "Swiss cheese fruit." It resembles a pineapple and is composed of a cluster of green hexagonal scales. Unripe fruit is poisonous due to oxalic acid, but ripe fruit is edible and has a flavor described as a cross between banana and pineapple.

Keeping Monstera deliciosa alive and well in a home environment is not too difficult. It does best in soil that drains properly and is exposed to indirect light. The top inch of soil needs time to dry out in between waterings, so be sure to water regularly. Helping the plant climb can also promote the growth of its distinctive fenestrated leaves.

CHAPTER ONE
Reasons Why Monstera Deliciosa Fruit Is So Important To Grow

The distinctive leaves of Monstera deliciosa makes it a beautiful houseplant, but the main reason to cultivate it inside is for its cosmetic value. Cultivation of Monstera deliciosa for fruit production is less popular, particularly in non-native climates, because its fruit is regarded as a delicacy in some countries.

Important considerations for cultivating Monstera deliciosa fruit include the following:

• The fact that the fruit can be eaten is the most important thing about it.

Legend has it that as Monstera deliciosa ripens, its flesh takes on a tropical, sweet taste reminiscent of a cross between banana and pineapple. But you shouldn't eat the unripe fruit because it has oxalic acid.

• Ripe Monstera deliciosa fruit can be used in cooking in areas where the tree is cultivated for its edible fruit. Fresh or cooked, it adds flavor to savory and sweet foods and drinks alike.

• Cultural Significance: The fruit of the Monstera deliciosa tree is considered sacred in many indigenous communities, and the plant itself may have practical applications beyond its aesthetic appeal. It could, for instance, play a role in regional festivals or ceremonies.

• Gardeners, horticulturists, and botanists who enjoy the challenge of growing plants for both their beauty and their fruit-bearing capabilities may find growing Monstera deliciosa for its fruit to be an interesting hobby.

• Plant diversity: Monstera deliciosa may not have much of an impact on global biodiversity, but it can help local species thrive when left alone in natural habitats. For many different kinds of creatures, plants are essential because they provide both shelter and food.

Keep in mind that Monstera deliciosa is mostly cultivated for its eye-catching indoor plant appearance; the fruit is an added bonus for those curious about its unusual culinary qualities. Plants that are typically cultivated for their fruits in your area should be considered if you are intent on producing fruits.

Environmental And Climate-Related Needs

Warm and humid environments are ideal for the tropical Monstera deliciosa plant. To get the best results from growing this plant, try to recreate its native environment as much as possible. The ideal growing conditions for Monstera deliciosa are as follows:

• Temperatures ranging from 18°C to 27°C are ideal for Monstera deliciosa. Although it can withstand somewhat lower temperatures, it is best to keep it away from frost.

• Its ideal environment is indirect, bright light. Although it can survive in dim light, its growth rate can be slower and their distinctive fenestration—splits and holes—might not form as easily.

• High humidity is ideal for Monstera deliciosa. Humidity is usually rather high in its natural rainforest habitat. Ensuring a relative humidity of sixty percent or more is preferred. Misting the plant, putting a humidifier close by, or placing it on a tray with water and stones are all good ways to raise the humidity level.

• Pick a potting mix that adds moisture but drains easily. The ideal mixture would include pine bark, perlite, and peat. If you don't want to risk waterlogging your plant, check that it has drainage holes.

• Make sure the soil is always damp, but not soggy. In between waterings, make sure the top inch of soil dries off. Avoid letting the plant sit in standing water to prevent root rot, which can occur from overwatering.

• Feed the plant a balanced liquid fertilizer every two to four weeks throughout the spring and summer while it is actively growing. When the plant's growth slows down in the fall and winter, fertilizer should be reduced or eliminated.

• As soon as the Monstera deliciosa outgrows its pot, repot it. You may manage the plant's size and shape by pruning it. Pruning on a regular basis can also promote bushier growth.

• As a climbing plant, Monstera deliciosa thrives when given a hand. A moss pole or trellis would be perfect for it to climb. Fenestrations in the leaves can flourish and the plant can grow more vertically as a result.

The particular needs of your Monstera may differ according to variables including your local weather, indoor circumstances, and the plant's size; so, these are only suggestions. To keep your Monstera deliciosa healthy and flourishing, it's important to check in on it often and make any necessary adjustments to its care routine.

CHAPTER TWO
Methods For Propagation

An enjoyable approach to make new plants or share existing ones is to propagate Monstera deliciosa, which can be done in a number of ways. Some typical ways that Monstera deliciosa is propagated are as follows:

• To propagate a cutting, you need at least one node (the point where a leaf attaches to the stem) and a few inches of stem. Verify that it has bloomed at least once. There is a better probability of success for cuttings if aerial roots are already present. Plant the cutting end in a potting mix that drains well and add rooting hormone (optional but can improve rooting).

In a matter of weeks, you should see root development as long as you maintain consistently wet soil. To keep the cutting moist, you can either put it in a humidity dome or cover it with a plastic bag.

• If at all feasible, select a fully grown stem that has aerial roots. Cut a tiny slit or slice off some of the stem's outer layer. Smother the exposed region with wet sphagnum moss and apply rooting hormone. To make a humid environment, wrap the moss in plastic. After the roots have taken hold, trim the stem down to the rooted area and plant it.

• When repotting an established plant, you have the option to divide it if it has several stems or shoots. Carefully detach the plant from its container and cut it into smaller pieces by separating its roots and stems. Every part needs to have its own set of stems, roots, and leaves. Transfer the cuttings to new pots and fill each with potting soil.

• Immerse the tip of a node-containing cutting in water. Make sure to change the water often to avoid stagnation and the growth of algae. Plant the cutting in soil as soon as its roots have grown a few inches.

• At the plant's base, Monstera deliciosa could develop suckers or offsets. Gently remove the offset and its roots from the parent plant before planting them in a separate container.

No matter what you do to propagate plants from cuttings, be sure to keep them in a warm, humid place. This facilitates the establishment of roots and the adaptation to their new environment. You may care for and maintain the young plants the same way you would an adult Monstera plant once they have roots and are actively growing.

Strategies For Planting And Transplantation

When you plant or transplant Monstera deliciosa, be sure to provide the plant with the ideal circumstances it needs to thrive in its new home. These are the steps to take when planting or repotting this tropical favorite:

Growing Delicious Monstera Plants:

• To avoid waterlogging, pick a pot with holes for drainage; Monstera plants dislike standing water. To ensure the plant has enough space to flourish, use a pot that is proportional to its size.

• Pick a potting mix that adds moisture but drains easily. The ideal mixture would include pine bark, perlite, and peat. For added air circulation, you can incorporate bark from orchids or coir from coconuts.

• Always check for roots before planting a cutting or juvenile Monstera. Allow the roots of a rooted cutting to mature to a minimum of a few inches in length before planting it.

• Return the Monstera to its original planting depth. To prevent decay, don't bury the stem too deeply.

• To help the Monstera roots take root, water them deeply after planting. It is important to make sure the soil is evenly moist, but not soggy.

• Set the Monstera plant in an area that gets plenty of indirect light after you plant it. Stay out of the sun as much as possible, particularly when the temperature is at its highest.

Repotting Delicious Monstera Plants:

• When the Monstera plant has outgrown its pot or when you see that the soil stays damp for a long time, it's a sign of inadequate drainage; in this case, transplant the plant.

• If you want to make the soil easier to work with when transplanting, water the plant a couple of days beforehand. Slide the plant out of the pot by gently tipping it. Tap the pot's base and sides to loosen the root ball if it's stubborn.

• Look for rot or disease indications on the roots. Using sharp, clean scissors or pruning shears, remove any roots that are damaged or rotting.

• Get a replacement pot with a diameter that's two inches bigger than the old one. It should have holes for water to drain.

• Fill the new pot with potting soil, then set the Monstera in the middle, making sure it sits at the same depth as before by adjusting the level.

• After transplanting, give the plant plenty of water to let the soil settle. To make sure the plant is adjusting properly, check the moisture level frequently in the first few weeks.

• To avoid stress, gradually adapt the plant to any changes in light conditions before transplanting it to a new site.

Never forget to keep an eye on your Monstera after planting or transplanting so you can tailor its care to its own requirements. When given the proper care, Monstera deliciosa can flourish and transform your indoor or outdoor space into a stunning landscape.

CHAPTER THREE
How To Water And Fertilize

To keep your Monstera deliciosa healthy, it is essential to water and fertilize it according to the plant's specific needs. When caring for your Monstera, keep these things in mind:

Gardening Advice:

• Keep to a regular watering schedule and let the soil dry out a full inch (2.5 cm) between each watering. Monstera does best in consistently moist soil, although excessive moisture might cause root rot.

• Water should be at room temperature; if feasible, it is best to let tap water sit for one day so that chlorine can evaporate. Certain pollutants found in municipal water systems can harm monstera plants.

• Root rot can occur if plants are overwatered. Never allow water to sit on top of a plant; instead, use a pot with drainage holes.

• Water the plant less frequently in the winter because its growth slows down at that time. See how the soil is holding up and make adjustments as needed.

• To find out if the soil is damp, stick your finger into it. You should water it when you feel the top inch become dry. Take into account the individual indoor conditions when adjusting the frequency.

• Make sure the area around the plant is consistently humid. To help plants thrive in dry indoor environments, you can spritz them, use a humidity tray, or even set up a humidifier.

Hints on Fertilization:

• An ideal liquid fertilizer would have an equal proportion of nitrogen, phosphorous, and potassium. You can water Monstera deliciosa with a half- or quarter-strength solution of a general-purpose fertilizer.

• At intervals of two to four weeks during the spring and summer, fertilize your plants. When the plant's growth slows down in the fall and winter, fertilizer should be reduced or eliminated.

• Make sure to follow the manufacturer's directions while diluting fertilizer. An excess of fertilizer can cause soil salts to accumulate, which can harm plants.

• Plants that have just been transplanted or placed in pots could be more vulnerable to the effects of fertilizers. Do not add fertilizers until they have adjusted to their new home.

• Foliar feeding involves spraying a diluted liquid fertilizer directly onto the leaves to supply nutrients. This can be done on occasion. But fertilizing soil should be your first priority.

• See how the plant fares after being fertilized. Fertilize less frequently or more heavily if you see leaf yellowing or other symptoms of fertilizer burn.

You should keep in mind that variables such as the plant's size, the pot's capacity, the surrounding environment, and the fertilizer in question can all affect the specifics of each plant's care needs. Monitor your Monstera deliciosa's condition on a regular basis to determine how much water and fertilizer it requires.

Approaches To Pruning

Monstera deliciosa can be trained to stay within its desired size, shape, and aesthetic with regular pruning. Monstera deliciosa can be pruned in the following ways:

• Use clean, sharp pruning shears to remove diseased or damaged leaves from near the main stem. In addition to making the plant seem better, this also helps the plant's vital energy go to its healthier areas.

• Sometimes, Monstera deliciosa can grow rather tall and narrow. When it starts to take over its room, it's time to prune it back to a manageable size.

At a point slightly above a leaf node, trim stems to the desired length.

• To achieve a bushier look, just cut off the very ends of the stems. This makes the plant look fuller by encouraging it to branch out and grow new growth from lower nodes.

• Monstera, when grown in damp environments, frequently develops aerial roots. You can either leave the roots as is or cut them down to size if you think they detract too much from the plant's aesthetic.

• You might want to consider cutting back the long, lanky stems of your Monstera to a leaf node if they have few leaves. This encourages neater, more aesthetically pleasing development.

• You can propagate plants by using cut stems that have nodes. To propagate the plants, just soak the cuttings in water or plant them in soil.

• Cut back any stems that are leaning too far in one direction or are getting in the way. As a result, the plant receives more oxygen and more light from the sky.

• When repotting your Monstera, it's a good opportunity to thin out any overgrown roots and shape the plant so it fits neatly into its new pot.

Some Pruning Thoughts:

• To make clean cuts with minimal danger of infection, always use sharp, clean pruning shears or scissors.

• If you want your plants to grow back faster after a pruning, do it in the spring or summer when they're actively growing.

• Don't Overprune: Although pruning has its benefits, it's best to keep the plant at a third of its original size to avoid stress.

• Regularly evaluate the rate of growth of your Monstera and make adjustments to its pruning schedule as needed.

• Think About the Plant's Natural Form: When pruning monstera deliciosa, try to keep part of the plant's naturally wild and tropical look.

You can keep your Monstera deliciosa looking healthy and beautiful by using these pruning procedures. Think about the plant's unique requirements and your personal aesthetic preferences when deciding how often and severely to prune.

CHAPTER FOUR
Management And Prevention Of Diseases

The care of Monstera deliciosa must include the prevention and management of diseases. Although Monstera plants are often resilient, there are a few problems to which they are vulnerable. To keep Monstera deliciosa healthy and disease-free, follow these guidelines:

Preventing Disease:

• To avoid root damage caused by waterlogging, make sure the pot has drainage holes. Promote healthy aeration by working with soil that drains well.

• Be sure to water the plant well, but wait for the top inch of soil to dry out in between. Keep the soil moist at all times to prevent the formation of fungi, therefore be careful not to overwater.

• When cutting or propagating, make sure to use clean, sharp pruning tools to avoid spreading diseases. Make sure to disinfect tools after each usage in case you notice any problems.

• Before adding additional plants to your collection, make sure to quarantine them for a few weeks. This aids in keeping infections and pests at bay.

• More humidity is ideal for Monstera deliciosa. Keeping things damp can ward off some bugs and fungal problems. If necessary, use a humidifier or a tray to retain moisture.

• Make sure there is plenty of airflow surrounding the plant. To keep it healthy and free of fungal illnesses, don't put it in a damp, stagnant spot.

• Check for pests, infections, or stress on a regular basis by examining your Monstera. Problems can be quickly addressed if caught early.

Treatment of Illnesses:

• Remove the plant from its container, remove diseased roots, and repot it in new, well-draining soil if you see symptoms of root rot (such as wilting, yellowing, or mushy roots).

• To address fungal problems like powdery mildew or leaf spots, it's recommended to increase air circulation, not water from above, and follow the instructions on the label when using fungicides.

• Monstera can be impacted by common pests such as mealybugs, spider mites, and scale insects. Beem oil or insecticidal soap can be used to keep pests at bay. To stop the infestation from spreading, remove the plants that are seriously damaged.

• To stop the spread of illness, cut off any diseased stems or leaves. Take care to dispose of the cut materials correctly.

• Neem oil can kill insects and fungi. For effective treatment and prevention of common pests and fungal concerns, try using a neem oil solution.

• To stop the spread of illness, quarantine sick plants separately from healthy ones.

• To make things less inviting for pests and diseases, you might want to try changing things around in terms of light, humidity, or temperature if problems continue.

Whenever you use a fungicide or insecticide, be sure to follow the directions on the label. Quick action is required in the event of an issue so that it does not spread to other plants in your collection. Disease prevention and management for Monstera deliciosa requires regular care, monitoring, and prompt intervention.

Fruit Ripeness Indicators And Harvesting Methods

Fruits of the Monstera deliciosa tree are distinctive and often called "Swiss cheese fruit" because of their shape and size. For the best flavor, you need to know when and how to pick the fruit. Here are some ways to tell when Monstera deliciosa fruit is ready and when to pick it:

Indications That Fruit Is Ready to Be Eaten:

• As the fruit ripens, its color changes from green to a creamier or even yellowish hue. The aroma of ripe fruits is usually rather pleasant.

• The fruit's fleshy segments will become visible when the hexagonal scales begin to separate. The fruit is obviously ripe for picking at this point.

• The pleasant aroma of ripe Monstera fruit is sometimes compared to that of pineapple and banana. The aroma of ripe fruit is a reliable sign that the fruit is ready to be eaten.

• As it ripens, the fruit becomes slightly pliable when touched. To find out if the scales are giving, press gently on them.

• The fruit is easier to remove from the plant when it is ripe. When picking fruit from a stem doesn't require much effort, it's probably ready to be picked.

Approaches to Harvesting:

• Remove the fruit from the plant using clean pruning shears. Cut around the stem's base so as not to harm neighboring plant sections.

• Hold off on harvesting the fruit until it reaches full ripeness on the plant. The optimal texture and taste are guaranteed in this way.

• Do not pick fruit that is still green and lacks the telltale changes in color; such fruit is neither completely ripe nor tasty.

• Be gentle when handling the fruit so as not to bruise it or damage its scales. Marks are plainly visible on the fruit's fragile skin.

• It takes time for Monstera deliciosa fruit to ripen. Wait until you see several ripeness indicators before picking.

• Occasionally, Monstera fruit can be plucked off the plant when it is still green, and then left to ripen. The fruit will continue to ripen if placed in a warm, dark spot.

• To avoid skin irritation from plant sap, it is recommended to wear gloves when harvesting, especially if you have sensitive skin.

Keep in mind that ripe Monstera deliciosa fruit may be hard to come by because the plant is not widely cultivated for its fruit in many areas. If you're lucky enough to get your hands on some Monstera fruit, make sure to eat it in moderation. The unripe fruit is toxic due to oxalic acid.

Summary

The Swiss cheese plant, or Monstera deliciosa, is an interesting and well-liked tropical plant with fenestrated leaves and, under ideal circumstances, the ability to produce tasty, unusual fruit.

Monstera deliciosa requires special attention when grown, including a controlled environment with just the correct amount of light, humidity, water, and fertilizer.

You can grow more Monstera plants or share them with others by using propagation techniques including stem cuttings, air layering, or division.

Disease prevention and management, in addition to pruning, are critical components of plant health maintenance that assist control the plant's size, shape, and general look.

It takes time and awareness of ripening indicators including color change, smell, and texture to harvest Monstera deliciosa fruit. The best fruit is picked when it is at its peak ripeness, so be careful and use clean pruning shears.

Consistent care, monitoring the plant's needs, and adjusting your techniques accordingly are the keys to cultivating Monstera deliciosa for either attractive foliage or fruit, or both. Monstera deliciosa, when given the proper care, may blossom into an eye-catching and fruitful plant for any garden, whether indoors or out.

THE END

Printed in Great Britain
by Amazon

47958709R00030